Wolves
THE OFFICIAL 2020 ANNUAL

Written by Paul Berry

Designed by Abbie Groom,
Synaxis Design Consultancy Ltd

A Grange Publication

© 2019. Published by Grange Communications Ltd., Edinburgh, under licence from Wolverhampton Wanderers Football Club. Printed in the EU.

Photographs © AMA Sport Photo Agency – Sam Bagnall, Dave Bagnall, Matt Ashton, James Baylis, Robbie Jay Barratt; SM2 Studio – Stuart Manley, Shaun Mallen; PA Images and the Wolves Archive.

ISBN: 978-1-913034-35-1

Contents

06   Nuno in Numbers

08   2018/19 Season Review

18   The Cup that so Almost Cheered

20   Si Señor!

22   Premier Pix

24   He's Joao Moutinho

26   Conor Goes Back to School

28   Quiz: The Numbers Game

29   Quiz: A Premier Wordsearch

30   What's Up, Doc?

34   Wolves Women: Pricey's Points of View

36   Wolves in China

38   Young Wolves

40   Wolfie's Fun Page

41   Quiz: Who Are Ya?

42   Academy: Homegrown Hero

43   Academy: Three to Watch

46   King Henry!

48   Wolves Foundation

50   New Signing: Jesus Vallejo

51   New Signing: Patrick Cutrone

52   Wolves Going for Esports Gold

54   Pat And Dave's Wolves Museum Mini-Tour

56   New Signing: Pedro Neto

57   New Signing: Bruno Jordao

58   Player Profiles

60   A Kit Fit for the Prem!

61   Quiz Answers

62   Where's Wolfie?

Wolves Head Coach Nuno Espirito Santo has enjoyed a fantastic first two years in the Molineux hotseat.

Storming to the Championship title was followed by a hugely impressive return to the Premier League, a seventh placed finish securing a place in the Europa League, not to mention an exciting run to the FA Cup semi-finals.

All of this has combined to make Nuno an extremely popular figure among the Wolves faithful, who have relished seeing their team operating towards the higher end of the top division for the first time in almost 40 years.

Here we take a look at some of the numbers which have underpinned such an exhilarating two years!

NUNO
IN NUMBERS

56

The number of games won by Wolves during Nuno's first 100 at the helm, the best win percentage of any manager in the club's history.

7

Seventh place finish for Wolves was the highest in the top division since John Barnwell's side came in at sixth in the 1979/80 campaign.

16

The number of points Wolves took off the top six teams during the 2018/19 Premier League season.

21

Number of players used by Wolves during the Premier League season, of which only two were brought on only for a few seconds in the final game. Much credit has to go to Nuno's backroom staff behind the scenes.

154

The number of goals scored by Nuno's team during his first 100 games in charge.

39

Wolves' tie against Crusaders in the Europa League was the first in European competition since the UEFA Cup clash with PSV Eindhoven, almost 39 years previously.

21

It had been 21 years since Wolves had reached an FA Cup semi-final, and against Watford they got so close to reaching a final for the first time in 59 years.

31,030

Wolves' average Premier League attendance for the 2018/19 campaign, the highest since 1970

1

The number of times Nuno has celebrated a goal by running up the touchline and diving into the melee

57

Wolves' tally of league points in their first season back, the third highest of a newly promoted team in the Premier League era

Everton / Leicester / Manchester City / Sheffield Wednesday

D   L   D   W

AUGUST
2018

Wolves headed into their first season in the Premier League for some seven years with some more exciting signings added to the squad, including Portuguese internationals Rui Patricio and Joao Moutinho, Mexican striker Raul Jimenez, Spanish full back Jonny Otto, Belgian international Leander Dendoncker and speed merchant Adama Traore.

A pre-season which included trips to Switzerland and Germany, and a friendly against eventual Champions League semi-finalists Ajax at Walsall, was rounded off with a 2-1 win against Villarreal at Molineux.

The stadium was then positively crackling with expectation for the opening day, and the visit of an Everton side expected to provide a stern barometer for what was to follow.

Ruben Neves and Raul Jimenez were on target in a lively 2-2 draw, and Wolves would also share the spoils in their second home game, albeit this one against reigning Premier League champions Manchester City.

In between times a first defeat of the season came, albeit in undeserved fashion, away at Leicester, but Wolves rounded off August with a 2-0 win at Sheffield Wednesday in the EFL Cup.

MOMENT OF THE MONTH:
Ruben Neves firing home Wolves' first goal of the season from a fantastic free kick.

SEPTEMBER

2018

The first day of September heralded Wolves' first Premier League win for some six and a half years, and all thanks to record summer signing and supersub Adama Traore.

After a game at the Olympic Stadium in which Wolves had traded chances with hosts West Ham, Traore burst clear in the third minute of added time to produce the clinical finish which got the season up and running.

It would go on to be an excellent September for Wolves, establishing themselves in the top flight and showing they could very much thrive at the highest level, with Head Coach Nuno landing the Manager of the Month award at its conclusion.

Home victories over Burnley and Southampton, both accompanied by clean sheets, were sandwiched either side of an impressive 1-1 draw against Manchester United at Old Trafford where Joao Moutinho capped his growing influence with his first Wolves goal.

Indeed the only blip in the landscape came with a penalty shootout exit in the EFL Cup, as two much-altered Wolves and Leicester teams – 17 combined changes in total – played out a goalless draw in the second round tie at Molineux.

MOMENT OF THE MONTH:

It has to be the last gasp Adama Traore goal which secured the first Premier League win of the season in the last seconds at West Ham.

OCTOBER
2018

After such a fantastic September, it was going to take some topping in October, and unfortunately it didn't quite happen.

In football terms it was a very quiet month, with only three Premier League fixtures as a result of the second international 'break' of the season.

The month still started well enough, a win at Crystal Palace making it six unbeaten in the league and four wins out of five.

The only goal of the game came courtesy of a revitalised Matt Doherty, with a fantastic late double save from Rui Patricio ensuring Wolves posted their most impressive top flight run for 39 years.

It was after that when Wolves' fortunes worsened, surprisingly beaten 2-0 at home by an impressive Watford and then finishing the month with a 1-0 defeat in a scrappy encounter at Brighton.

MOMENT OF THE MONTH:

Is there a Doc in the house? Matt Doherty's first ever Premier League goal was a crucial one, securing victory at Crystal Palace to continue Wolves' fine start to the season.

L D L L

NOVEMBER
2018

After successive defeats, the prospect of back-to-back fixtures with North London giants Tottenham and Arsenal might not have been top of most wishlists for the bid to return to winning ways.

Especially when Wolves found themselves 3-0 down against Spurs just after the hour mark.

But from there, penalties from Ruben Neves and Raul Jimenez saw Wolves go mighty close to a spectacular comeback, which they followed up by going equally close to a win at the Emirates.

It needed a late Henrikh Mkhitaryan equaliser four minutes from time to cancel out Ivan Cavaleiro's early opener to deny Wolves all three points against the Gunners.

Unfortunately however, the final two games of the month saw memories revived of some disappointing Novembers past, successive defeats against Huddersfield and Cardiff extending the team's winless run to six games.

MOMENT OF THE MONTH:

Arsenal keeper and defenders on the floor, and Ivan Cavaleiro celebrating, as Wolves took the lead after a well-worked goal at the Emirates.

DECEMBER 2018

This Wolves side have shown they have the welcome habit of bouncing back, and, after back-to-back defeats, six without a win and a goal down to Chelsea just before the hour mark, bounce back is exactly what they did.

Quickfire goals from Raul Jimenez and Diogo Jota, a sign of what their partnership would deliver over the rest of the season, secured a famous win and Wolves' first over a top six side. There would be many more to follow!

The win was followed by two more, Matt Doherty's last gasp goal securing three points at Newcastle, and a professional job carried out on Bournemouth with a 2-0 victory at Molineux.

In-form league leaders Liverpool proved too hot to handle next up, claiming a 2-0 win, after which Wolves had to come from behind to draw at Fulham on Boxing Day.

But they would finish the month as they began it, overcoming one of the big boys and rounding off a sensational 2018 with a sensational win at Wembley, a second half masterclass sweeping Tottenham aside.

MOMENT OF THE MONTH:

It's Conor Coady with the celebration, but Helder Costa had just scored, crowning a fantastic Wolves comeback to overcome Tottenham at Wembley.

JANUARY

2019

In terms of the Premier League, January was very much a 'month of two halves' for Wolves.

After the high of beating Spurs at Wembley to end 2018, the New Year got off to a disappointing start with a home defeat against Crystal Palace, and then 3-0 reverse at title-chasing Manchester City, albeit having lost Willy Boly to a 19th minute red card with the score at 1-0.

One of the most dramatic games of the season saw Wolves lead 2-0 and 3-2 against Leicester only to get pegged back again on 87 minutes, before Diogo Jota struck a famous winner deep into added time.

There followed a far more comfortable, and frighteningly efficient, 3-0 dismissal of West Ham, completing Wolves' first league double of the season and first ever over the Hammers.

January also saw Wolves' FA Cup campaign off and running, an impressive 2-1 win over Liverpool in the third round the prelude to a dramatic escape act in the fourth, goals from Raul Jimenez and Matt Doherty ensuring Wolves avoided becoming one of the many notches on Shrewsbury Town's giant-killing bedpost!

MOMENT OF THE MONTH:

One of those truly memorable afternoons, as Diogo Jota's injury time goal settles a rollercoaster ride to clinch a 4-3 win against Leicester, the same scoreline as the previous Premier League fixture at Molineux.

13

FEBRUARY
2019

One of the most impressive away performances of the season saw Everton comfortably dispatched 3-1 at Goodison Park on the first weekend of February, allowing Wolves to chalk up a third successive Premier League win for the second time in the season.

Newcastle on a Monday night proved more of a stern challenge, and it needed another late show against the Toon to take something from the game, Willy Boly's late header earning a point.

Bournemouth on the road provided another 1-1 draw, before the month finished in disappointing fashion as Huddersfield, who

had taken one point from a possible 42 since beating Wolves in November, produced a last gasp goal to complete the double over Nuno's team.

Wolves continued to make progress in the FA Cup, albeit after another slight scare when going 2-1 behind to Shrewsbury in the fourth round replay, but Matt Doherty's second of the game and an Ivan Cavaleiro winner booked a place in the last 16.

A trip to Ashton Gate to face a Bristol City side unbeaten in 15 and boasting nine successive wins looked a lively one, but Cavaleiro was again the man on the spot to take Wolves through.

MOMENT OF THE MONTH:

With apologies to Leander Dendoncker, whose excellent finish at Everton capped a superb Wolves performance, the appearance of a Black Cat to hold up the game in the second half was a source of great amusement!

MARCH
2019

Just three Premier League fixtures in the month of March and Wolves completed the full set of results with a win, a draw and a defeat.

In that order as well!

It all started well enough with the in-form strike pairing of Diogo Jota and Raul Jimenez bagging a quickfire goal apiece in the 16th and 18th minutes to secure a 2-0 win against Cardiff.

The draw which came next could easily have been a win, at Chelsea as well, with Eden Hazard's added time effort denying Wolves victory after Jimenez had bagged the opener.

And while March finished on a losing note away at Burnley, the highlight of the month had already happened, in the FA Cup quarter finals.

On a truly electric night at Molineux, it was those two again – Jimenez and Jota – with the goals which overcame the might of Manchester United and saw Wolves through to the semi finals.

MOMENT OF THE MONTH:

Diogo Jota's second goal against Manchester United, who raised the roof at Molineux, and sparked some great celebrations after full time.

W L L D W W

APRIL
2019

The month of April was, perhaps understandably, centred around the small matter of a trip to Wembley to take on Watford in the semi-finals of the FA Cup.

For so long, Wolves were knocking on the door of a first appearance in the final for 59 years, but fell agonisingly short, seeing a 2-0 lead 11 minutes from time extinguished, including an added time penalty.

And then substitute Gerard Deulofeu, who had launched the Watford comeback with their first goal, broke Wolves hearts with the extra time winner.

Wolves had gone into the game in great heart, buoyed by another excellent 2-1 home win against Manchester United, but how they would respond after the FA Cup heartbreak would shape the remainder of the season.

Initially it wasn't great with defeat at Southampton and a home draw against Brighton, but another stunning victory over one of the big boys, Arsenal, set up a revenge mission against Watford.

On this occasion the Wolves managed to sting the Hornets, a 2-1 win putting them in sight of the seventh-placed finish that would open the door to European football.

MOMENT OF THE MONTH:

It would ultimately prove in vain, but Raul Jimenez scoring at Wembley and donning a wrestling mask of his friend Sin Cara was a memory which will stand the test of time.

W L

MAY
2019

Victory at Watford, and results elsewhere, offered Wolves the carrot that a win against Fulham in the final home game of the season would push them very close to guaranteeing seventh place, and the potential of a place in the Europa League.

It proved a tight afternoon against a Fulham side which had improved under the stewardship of Scott Parker, but, in front of Sin Cara, Wolves finally 'wrestled' the advantage and Leander Dendoncker's excellent finish 15 minutes from time secured the points.

There followed the usual lap of appreciation after another excellent Molineux season, but there was still one assignment remaining, the trip to a Liverpool side who needed to win – and Manchester City to slip up – to win their first top flight title in 29 years.

Wolves gave another fine account of themselves at Anfield, but a Sadio Mane brace earned the points for the Reds, albeit it wasn't enough for the title after City coasted to three points and top spot once again at Brighton.

MOMENT OF THE MONTH:

Wolves Head Coach Nuno Espirito Santo receiving an Honorary Doctor of Sport degree from the University of Wolverhampton prior to kick off against Fulham.

THE CUP THAT SO ALMOST
CHEERED...

It had been a long time since Wolves enjoyed a good FA Cup run. Twenty-one years since the semi-final defeat against Arsenal at Villa Park, and 59 since the last final, the 3-0 win against Blackburn. For so long, it looked like that famous phrase 'your name's on the cup' was going to apply to the gold and black class of 2018/19.

Overcoming Liverpool in the third round, a last gasp equaliser at Shrewsbury, epic victory against Manchester United, and all during a season when the legendary Bill Slater, the last Wolves captain to lift the famous old trophy, had passed away. In the end it just wasn't quite to be, but, despite the crushing disappointment of the semi-final defeat against Watford at Wembley, there was still so much to be proud of during the exciting run.

ROUND 3:

Wolves 2
Liverpool 1

On the night when Wolves paid tribute to the great Bill Slater, the current team produced a fitting tribute of their own thanks to an impressive win.

Raul Jimenez put Wolves in front before half time and then, after Divock Origi drew Liverpool level shortly after the interval, a typically spectacular strike from Ruben Neves proved decisive.

ROUND 4:

Shrewsbury 2
Wolves 2

Wow this was close! After a tight first half Wolves found themselves two goals down with 15 minutes remaining as their Shropshire neighbours, managed by former Molineux captain Sam Ricketts, sensed a famous giant-killing.

But Raul Jimenez pulled a goal back, and Wolves broke Shrews hearts when Matt Doherty headed home an Adama Traore cross with 93 minutes on the clock.

R4 REPLAY:

Wolves 3
Shrewsbury 2

The replay wasn't all plain sailing either, with Matt Doherty topping and tailing the first half scoring for Wolves, only for his second goal to be an equaliser thanks to efforts from James Bolton and Josh Laurent for the visitors.

But Wolves made it consecutive home wins in the FA Cup for the first time since 2006 when Ivan Cavaleiro burst through to notch the winner midway through the second half.

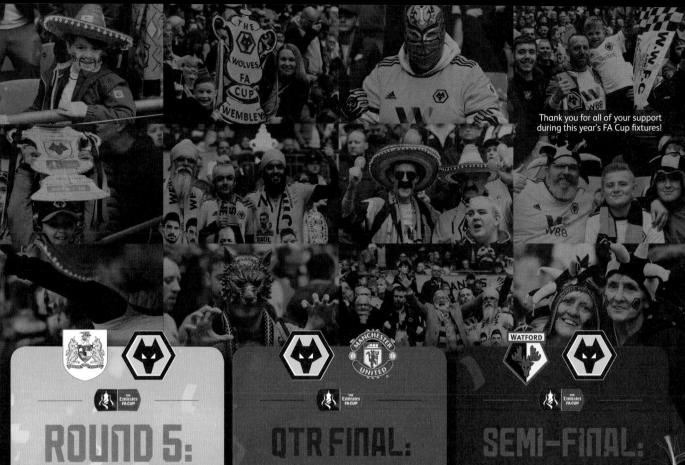

ROUND 5:

Bristol City 0
Wolves 1

A very tough draw on paper, with the in-form and fired-up Championship side on a run of nine successive wins heading into this Sunday afternoon tussle.

Ivan Cavaleiro's neat finish just before the half hour mark proved the only goal of the game, but it needed some fine goalkeeping from John Ruddy and battling defence in the closing stages to seal the win.

QTR FINAL:

Wolves 2
Manchester United 1

Oh what a night! Molineux was rocking, the atmosphere crackling, and the Wolves players responded with an incredible performance to book their place in the semi finals.

They were already the better side by the time strike duo Raul Jimenez and Diogo Jota found the net on 70 and 76 minutes respectively, and a late strike from Marcus Rashford was merely a consolation.

SEMI-FINAL:

Watford 3
Wolves 2

The ecstasy. And then the agony. In search of a first FA Cup Final in 59 years, Wolves were in charge at Wembley with Matt Doherty's first half header and Raul Jimenez's great volley. But substitute Gerard Deulofeu pulled one back with a superb goal, Troy Deeney fired home an added time penalty, and Deulofeu provided the winner in extra time. A bitter pill to swallow at the end of such a magnificent cup campaign – now on to the next one!

¡SÍ, SEÑOR!

GIVE THE BALL TO RAUL & HE WILL SCORE

WHAT A FIRST SEASON AT WOLVES IT WAS FOR RAUL JIMENEZ, WHOSE LOAN SPELL FROM BENFICA WAS TURNED INTO A PERMANENT DEAL FOR A CLUB RECORD FEE.

The man from Mexico scored a fantastic 17 goals in all competitions, as well as seven assists, and was voted the Players' Player of the Year at the end of the season.

Jimenez also showed he can score all different types of goal, so here the Wolves Annual looks back at his top ten efforts – and their variety – from a spectacular debut 2018/19 season.

THE HEADER

Jimenez scored from three headers during the season, two of which came against Everton, including his first Wolves goal on the season's opening day from a pin-point Ruben Neves cross.

THE CHEEKY ONE

Placement is also vital for any goal-grabbing striker, and Jimenez's low effort against Spurs at Wembley wasn't the most powerful, but nestled perfectly in the bottom corner of the net.

THE SIDEFOOT

An intricate side-footed finish, first-time, to convert Matt Doherty's cross for the only goal of the game against Burnley.

THE RUN

Jimenez has also shown he can do a lot of great work off the ball, and also make powerful runs, as shown in the FA Cup win against Liverpool when he broke from just inside the Reds' half and kept his composure to put Wolves in front.

THE PENALTY

Coolness personified in tucking home this penalty against Tottenham, a feat he repeated in the away game at Bournemouth later in the season.

THE DINK

Having already shown a great first-time flicked finish against West Ham, Jimenez also executed the 'dink' just a few minutes later, deftly chipping Hammers keeper Lukasz Fabianski for his only left-footed strike of the season.

THE POWER

You don't save those! Jimenez latches onto a fine ball from Morgan Gibbs-White and smashes in a low shot which leaves Chelsea keeper Kepa Arrizabalaga floundering.

ON THE TURN

It looked like there was no option available for the Mexican maestro when crowded out inside the Manchester United penalty area, but he produced a superb swivel and shot to outwit Sergio Romero and break the deadlock in the FA Cup tie.

THE TAP-IN

Positioning can often be as important as power, and here Jimenez was perfectly placed to tap home after Diogo Jota flashed the ball across the box.

THE VOLLEY

The man who would then wear the mask showed all his technical ability for his second Wembley goal of the season, controlling a Matt Doherty cross on his chest before firing home a volley as he fell to the ground in the semi final against Watford.

PREMIER PIX!

What a season for thousands of Wolves fans who followed their team up and down the country with great success during the 2018/19 campaign.

For many steps along that journey, Stu Manley and Shaun Mallen from photographers SM2 Studio were alongside them, capturing mainly the joys of another fantastic nine months as Wolves marked their top-flight return in some style. So here are their Premier Pix - and we managed to sneak one or two in from the FA Cup as well.

HE'S JOAO
Moutinho

What a signing the midfield magician Joao Moutinho proved as the hugely experienced Portuguese international made his Premier League bow with Wolves at the age of 31.

He 'likes the vino' apparently too, albeit not so much during the season when his fitness and professionalism saw him appear in all 44 of Wolves' Premier League and FA Cup fixtures.

Moutinho's contribution and influence was immense, both on and off the pitch, and was rewarded by winning the Supporters' Player of the Year award at the end of the season.

Here we pay tribute to 'five foot seven of football heaven' and look at some of his numbers during the 2018/19 season.

182 DUELS WON

1863 PASSES

APPEARANCES: 44

minutes played: 3444

113 Tackles

8 ASSISTS

196 CROSSES

1 GOAL AGAINST MANCHESTER UNITED

ACCURATE 124 LONG BALLS

84 CHANCES CREATED

264 RECOVERIES

40 interceptions

Conor goes BACK TO SCHOOL!

ARE SCHOOLDAYS REALLY THE BEST DAYS OF YOUR LIFE?

We caught up with **Wolves** captain Conor Coady, to dig into his memory bank about his time as a student! Conor went to Rainford High School in Saint Helens, and here are some of his memories.

FAVOURITE SUBJECT?

"I'd say that was always PE. But I guess for a footballer that's an easy one to go with.

Another subject I really enjoyed was history. I found it interesting to find out what had gone on in the past.

WERE YOU GOOD AT EVERYTHING IN PE?

"I was OK at sport, but not as good as some footballers I know. Ryan Bennett is good at everything, absolutely everything!

Whatever sport it is, Benno is there. For me football was always the main one and the one I was best at."

WORST SUBJECT?

"Maths. Didn't like that one at all. Probably because I was rubbish at it. I did alright in all my exams to be fair but maths was one I struggled with.

WERE YOU A GOOD BOY AT SCHOOL?

"I wasn't naughty or anything like that. My school reports were OK as well and my Mum and Dad were always happy with what came back. I was a good boy, never doing anything wrong. I was already at Liverpool's Academy when I was at school and we were told there would be problems if we got into trouble at school. So I stayed away from it!

My wife Amie was at the same school, and she'd probably tell you I was the teacher's pet!"

WHAT WOULD YOUR TEACHERS SAY TO YOU NOW?

"I think they'd all be happy for me. To the question, 'What do you want to be when you grow up?' I would always say a footballer. And I think they knew I was serious because I was already at Liverpool. I behaved myself as well, so that meant I tended to get on well with all the teachers."

FAVOURITE TEACHER?

"I'd probably say Mr Machin, the PE teacher.

He was good. He ran our footy team as well but it was dead good as he let me pick the team. So all he would need to do is drive the bus!

I could pick all my mates and that so it worked out well."

WHAT WOULD YOU SAY TO YOUNG PEOPLE NOW ABOUT SCHOOL?

"I would say to make sure you enjoy it. You won't half miss it when you finish.

School is great, spending time with your mates and without any responsibilities, and then you go into a different world at the end of it.

Enjoy it as much as possible and get the most out of it because it does help you moving forward."

THE NUMBERS GAME

It is now 20 years since squad numbers were first brought into English football and so, for one of our quizzes, we are playing 'the numbers game'.

We have picked ten squad numbers from the last two decades, and given you a further three clues as to who the player is who wore that shirt.

If you identify the player from the number without any clues, award yourself four points; after one clue, three points; after two clues, two points; and after three clues, one point.

Tot up your score at the end to see just how good you are at playing the numbers game. Younger fans may be advised to ask Mum or Dad for help with this one!

1

#15
in Season
1999/2000

CLUE 1:
Versatile, featured in defence/midfield

CLUE 2:
Arrived at Wolves from Ipswich in 1997

CLUE 3:
Was an FA Cup winner with Coventry and Tottenham

2

#21
in Season
2001/2002

CLUE 1:
Would later move to the number 10 shirt

CLUE 2:
Scored Wolves' first ever Premier League winner

CLUE 3:
Was signed from Heart of Midlothian

3

#17
in Season
2003/2004

CLUE 1:
Once scored in five successive Wolves appearances

CLUE 2:
Player of the Year for this season

CLUE 3:
An international with Senegal

4

#16
in Season
2005/2006

CLUE 1:
Initially arrived on loan, before signing became permanent

CLUE 2:
Scored 58 goals in total for Wolves

CLUE 3:
Once notched a winner against Manchester United

5

#31
in Season
2007/2008

CLUE 1:
Played in all 46 of Wolves' league fixtures

CLUE 2:
Made his debut for Wolves in the play-offs the previous season

CLUE 3:
A Welsh international goalkeeper

6

#20
in Season
2009/2010

CLUE 1:
One of the summer signings after Wolves' Championship title win

CLUE 2:
Famed for a superb left foot

CLUE 3:
A Serbian international midfielder

7

#15
in Season
2011/2012

CLUE 1:
Made five appearances for Wolves

CLUE 2:
Arrived on loan in January

CLUE 3:
His parent club was Arsenal

8

#18
in Season
2013/2014

CLUE 1:
Occupied the defence for 44 out of 46 league games

CLUE 2:
Kenny Jackett's first Wolves signing

CLUE 3:
Captained the team to the League One title

9

#16
in Season
2015/2016

CLUE 1:
Arrived at Wolves in the summer of 2015

CLUE 2:
Made 35 league appearances in his first Molineux season

CLUE 3:
Would later captain the team to a promotion

7

#33
in Season
2017/2018

CLUE 1:
Scored on his competitive Wolves debut

CLUE 2:
Would finish with 12 goals for the season

CLUE 3:
Brazilian-born, he initially arrived on loan from Al-Hilal in Saudi Arabia

---

HOW DID YOU **SCORE?**

31-40 points:
Brilliant.
You are so good at numbers that you could be the next Carol Vorderman on Countdown. Take a bow.

21-30 points:
More than respectable.
You need a little bit of help with your maths, but you get there in the end.

11-20 points:
Hmm.
That number knowledge of Wolves over the last 20 years probably needs a bit of homework.

0-10 points:
Are you even a Wolves fan?
To the back of the class immediately!

A PREMIER WORDSEARCH!

It has become a regular feature in the Wolves Annual – our Monster Wordsearch! Can you do it faster this year than you did last?

It is very much a Premier wordsearch this year as, included within the grid, are all 20 teams who will be playing in the Premier League over the 2019/20 season, including of course Wolverhampton Wanderers!

Good luck!

- ☐ ARSENAL
- ☐ ASTON VILLA
- ☐ BOURNEMOUTH
- ☐ BRIGHTON AND HOVE ALBION
- ☐ BURNLEY
- ☐ CHELSEA
- ☐ CRYSTAL PALACE
- ☐ EVERTON
- ☐ LEICESTER CITY
- ☐ LIVERPOOL
- ☐ MANCHESTER CITY
- ☐ MANCHESTER UNITED
- ☐ NEWCASTLE UNITED
- ☐ NORWICH CITY
- ☐ SHEFFIELD UNITED
- ☐ SOUTHAMPTON
- ☐ TOTTENHAM HOTSPUR
- ☐ WATFORD
- ☐ WEST HAM UNITED
- ☐ WOLVERHAMPTON WANDERERS

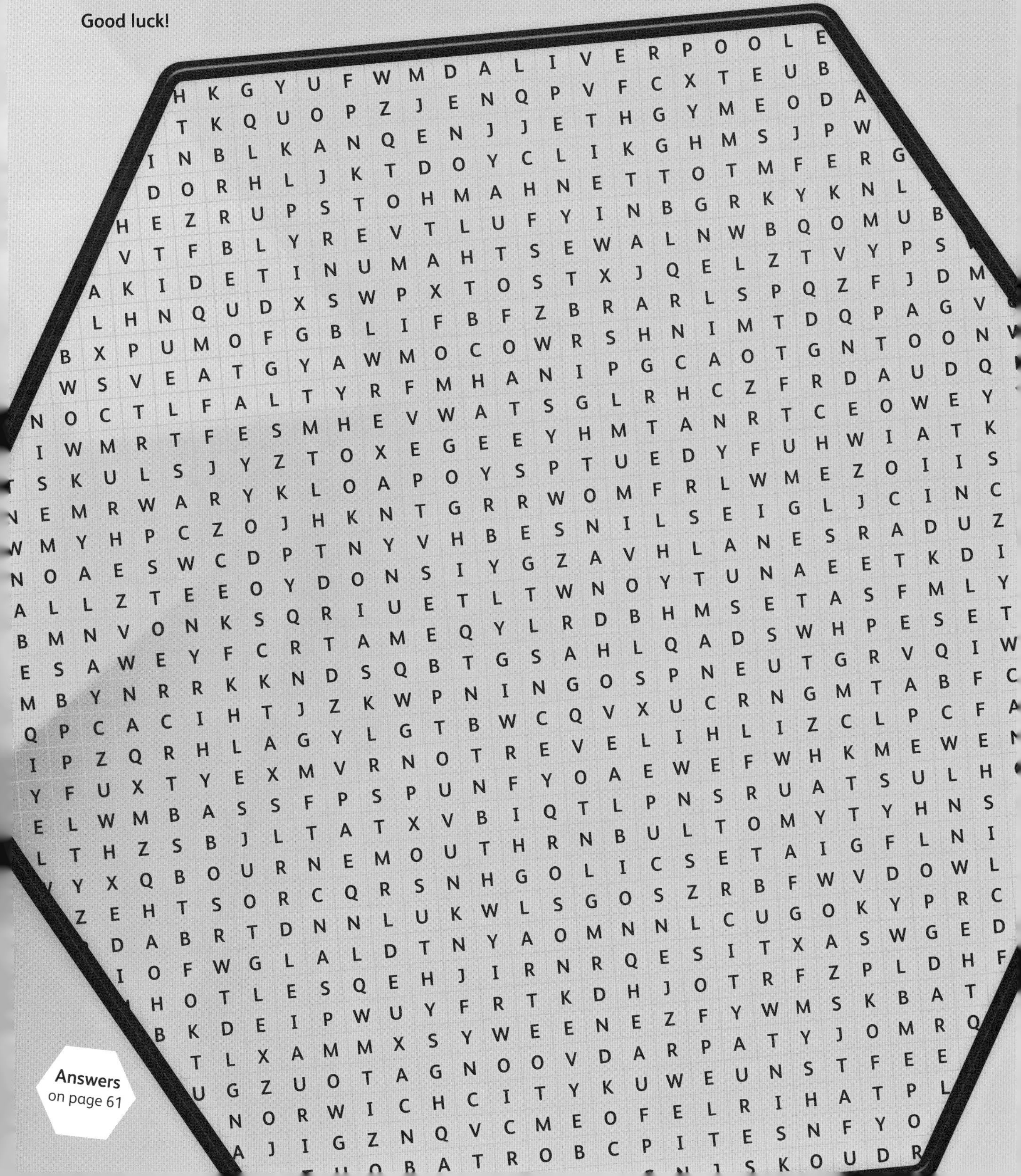

Answers on page 61

What's Up, Doc?

Wolves' longest-serving outfield player is now versatile defender Matt Doherty, who played so well against the club for Bohemians in a pre-season friendly in 2010, he was promptly signed by Mick McCarthy!

Well known for his laid-back nature and dry sense of humour, 'Doc' is the perfect choice to give his thoughts on the mainstays of Wolves' fantastic 2018/19 season in the Premier League.

As well as football, Doc is a keen fan of cricket, a fun version of which is now played at the training ground when the players are on their 'down time' – you may find cricket featuring in some of these answers! Here is the Irishman's rundown on his Wolves team-mates...

RUI PATRICIO

Can he speak English? I don't know. He fits well in the dressing room and will chat Portuguese with the other guys. Once his English improves I will be able to banter with him a lot more. Most importantly he is a fantastic goalkeeper. He pulled off some saves to get us out of some difficult situations in his first season at Wolves. A vital last line of defence.

JOHN RUDDY

Right let's get this straight to start with. Ruddy is a bit of a spoofer. Do you know why? We had the top England cricketer Jimmy Anderson visit the training ground once, and Ruddy claims that he clean bowled him. That's not the case. Didn't happen. Ask anyone about it. What did happen was that I was bowling spin at Jimmy Anderson, and he just couldn't pick it. That's the real story. And it made John bitter. Apart from that, John's a good keeper and great guy, and a good golfer. Far better golfer than he is a cricketer. We have some good battles on the golf course and boy, he can hit the ball a long way.

WILL NORRIS

Cricket again. Will Norris is a goalkeeper, but he is the worst wicketkeeper at the club. How does that happen? Surely he should be good at that? Sometimes it is that bad that if I am batting, I will play and miss on purpose just to see what happens when the ball runs through to him. He just drops everything. I think you can see his confidence has completely gone at cricket now. We all just look at him and are thinking: 'What on earth is going on?' Worst wicketkeeper at the club, but probably got the best beard.

RYAN BENNETT

Benno is the biggest moaner at the club. For sure. But it doesn't really mean anything because whatever he moans about, he knows he has got to do it eventually. "I'm not doing that," he'll say. And then a few minutes later he'll do it. It's moaning for the sake of it, although I suppose we all do that a bit sometimes. On the pitch I play alongside Benno and we've got a good relationship. I sit beside him in the changing room, both at the training ground and on a matchday. Fair play to him he's had a great couple of seasons as well. We don't mind him moaning when he's doing the business on the pitch.

WILLY BOLY

Boly is strong. So strong. You know when you look at someone, and you know they must be strong, and then you get to find out properly. Sometimes he will get his fingers in my ribs, and it hurts so much that it gets to the point where I am almost angry with him. Like 'why would you even do that'? Because of how strong he is. Boly is good and gets involved in all the banter. I know he doesn't do many interviews but he's got good English so people maybe need to cotton on that he could do the interviews really. Although maybe no one wants to tell him that? A bit of a joker but a really really good player who has been pivotal to our success.

CONOR COADY

Still the teacher's pet. Still trying to be best mates with every manager he plays under. Sometimes I just want to fist fight him to be honest. He can be so annoying. Every single time we are travelling away from home, when I'm trying to get back in my room, he is there. He just wants to come in with me and start messing around or play-fighting or something. Well I'm not having that. So I end up just standing with him out in the corridor. I refuse to go in. There have been times when we have been stood in the corridor for 20 minutes and all the other lads are recording it from their keyholes because they know what is going on. He is the captain I suppose, and he picks me out a lot with his crossfield passes which is fair enough. But I still don't think that is enough to get around what he does. That's Coads for you.

JONNY OTTO

RUBEN VINAGRE

RUBEN NEVES

Jonny is like a little wall. He is quiet, but he is rock solid. Everyone can see the way he is built, not a pick on him. A very good professional and a very good player, especially as a right-footed player operating on the left. That shows how good he is, and I remember someone else doing that back in the day! An all-round nice guy.

Vinagre is my worst nightmare in training. In my position I have to come up against him quite a bit. The times when we are on the same time I will give a little fist pump as I am so relieved. He is so sharp, always at you and in your face. Sometimes it's nice to have just a quiet game in training but you know that's not going to happen when you are up against Vinagre. In all seriousness though it is good as it helps me improve. He is so tough to play against, that it makes my standards higher. He is already a good player but I think he will go on and be exceptional.

Neves likes his cricket. He is a surprisingly good wicketkeeper, and bowls wrist spin really well. I didn't even know cricket was a thing in Portugal. I'm not actually sure how legal his throwing action is, but he has got the lads out with it. And behind the stumps, he snaffles absolutely everything. He is always involved and up for the game. He'll come running in to see if we are playing. As for the football? Incredible. Another who picks me out on the pitch and it is such a good thing to have players like Neves in the team. As a wing back, if I make a big run into the opposition half, there are people who can see the pass and you know it's not going to be wasted. If he's not world-class already I'm sure he will be.

JOAO MOUTINHO

MORGAN GIBBS-WHITE

ROMAIN SAISS

A top professional, but also likes a joke at the right time. In training he is just so good. People ask me about Joao all the time, and it is so difficult to explain. Unless you are on the same pitch as him it is tough to understand just how good he is. Especially in tight areas. For someone who is fairly small, in defensive situations he always seems to get a toe in against the big guys as well. And he wins his fair share of headers. He is so experienced, and he is so clever. When he talks you just want to listen and learn from what he has to say. He has been through so much in the game and has that knowledge.

The young 'un! He is just so confident in life right now! Playing in the Premier League, playing for the England age-groups having already won the World Cup. It has all come pretty quickly for Morgan, but there is nowhere else really he could have gone with the talent that he has. He trains really well and has never looked out of place from the day he came into the first team group. He has kept his head down and is focused on what he wants to do and he knows he is getting an opportunity at a Premier League club – and also his local team – that not many players of his age enjoy. He has really grasped that and taken his chance.

Saiss...Mr Bean, you mean? That is what we call him, and he knows it. He just acts like Mr Bean sometimes, I don't think he has even seen the programme and the films. I sit opposite him on the coach and we'll both make stupid noises and look out of the corner of our eyes to see if the other one is looking. Kids' stuff really. He is good fun, like most of the lads. Everyone gets involved in the fun which is good. Saiss is top notch in that regard.

LEANDER DENDONCKER

IVAN CAVALEIRO

HELDER COSTA

I sit next to Leander at the dining table so a lot of our chat is about food. We look at what each other is eating and discuss it, seeing what carbs we have got on our plates. We are conscious about staying in shape, and we also share a fear of flying together as well. Both of us hate flying. Leander had a tough start when he got here and didn't play much, and some games wasn't even in the 18. But then from halfway through the season he was starting every week and doing really well. That just goes to show what sort of mental attitude he has to come through that and get himself a regular place in the team. He is also a regular for Belgium which is no easy thing given the talent that they have.

Me and Cav get on really well. We joke around a lot and he is a funny guy. Even with all the nationalities at Wolves, we seem to share the same kind of mentality and humour. We all like the same stuff, which doesn't always happen in a dressing room. Every day there was something funny going on between us, even just a comment or a look where you were searching for a reaction. Always messing about. I know he and Helder have left now, but I wish them both all the best and hope they tear it up.

I thought I linked up really well with Costa when we played with wingers and he was on the right. He is some player, one of the most talented I have seen. He is a bit quieter than Cav but still played his part in the dressing room and is a good guy. That is the thing with our dressing room, everyone that comes in seems to be a decent person. When you move to Wolves now, within a couple of days you must feel like you have been here for weeks or months it is so easy to settle in. Again sad to see him go.

RAUL JIMENEZ

DIOGO JOTA

ADAMA TRAORE

A legend in Mexico, and now in Wolverhampton too! Scored so many for us last season and is such a clever player. I'm not sure there are too many strikers who can do everything that he can on the pitch, and still chip in with goals as well. He works his socks off. Sometimes you play with strikers and you're not sure the ball is going to stick up there with them, but with Raul it does. And that is such a help. I have linked up well with him when I get forward. I think Wolves were seriously fortunate to get him in and the way we have played really seems to suit his game. He is so confident now, and I think that is everything in the game. Another nice guy, who hangs around with Jonny a fair bit.

Another who plays cricket. One of the worst fielders you have ever seen. He drops everything. He is costing people now and his lack of catching is starting to really affect the games. He drops the easiest of catches. Good job he can play football. In the second half of last season he was incredible. He scored a Premier League hat trick and was in the shake-up for Player of the Year which was fantastic given he had a bit of a tough start. He's in and amongst the Portugal squad, and gets himself involved at Wolves personality-wise.

We get on well. But, if Adama ever squeezes you...well let's just say you don't really want to be that person. You don't realise how strong he is, until he squeezes you. Every time I see him, or if I walk past him in the corridor, we never pass each other without something happening. We just have to say something to each other, even if it's a couple of words of abuse! He is that strong he scares me a bit to be honest. On the pitch I could watch Adama all day long. He has that something about him, with that frightening pace. I know he might be battling with me for the wing back spot and that will be good for us to put pressure on each other.

HOME SINCE 1889.

WOLVES WOMEN:
PRICEY'S POINTS OF VIEW

Wolves Women headed into the 2019/20 campaign in positive mood, having gone so close to promotion from Division 1 Midlands as they finished runners-up the season before.

This confidence was also buoyed by closer relationships developed at Wolves, with the ladies now training at the club's Compton Park headquarters twice a week, and players of all ages no longer having to pay subscription fees. This decision was expected to remove any existing barriers between young girls and their hopes of playing football, at a time when England's participation in the 2019 World Cup Finals had ignited fresh interest in the sport.

So who are the Wolves Women? Which players are aiming to lead the club into an exciting new era? There is no one better than experienced skipper Anna Price to tell us more – so we asked her! Here's a quick rundown on the Wolves Women!

HOLLIE HOGAN
NUMBER 10

In the nicest possible sense of the word, Hollie is an absolute beast. And that is a compliment. Hollie takes no messing on the pitch, and if it means going through the opponent to get the ball, then that is what she will do. In training as well! Hollie also loves a header.

JESS JENNINGS
WINGER

The youngest player in our squad, and one of the most skilful. Jess is another who is fairly quiet off the pitch but becomes really confident on it when she can express her skills. Loves to take a player on and beat them, and if she beats them once, more than likely she will try and beat them again!

LOWRI WALKER
STRIKER/NUMBER 10

Lowri was this season's poster girl by being featured in the publicity photographs for Wolves' new kit. She was already famous for producing the bicycle kick that confirmed a great victory for us against the Baggies, ending their unbeaten record on the final day of last season. Lowri wouldn't say boo to a goose off the pitch, but does the business when she is out there.

JADE CROSS
STRIKER

Emma's sister, and I think of her as the angry twin! She is quiet generally but doesn't half shout at her sister when they get on the pitch. They have some right barneys. I guess you can get away with it when you are so close as twins. Jade is a fantastic player, who was the league's top goalscorer last season.

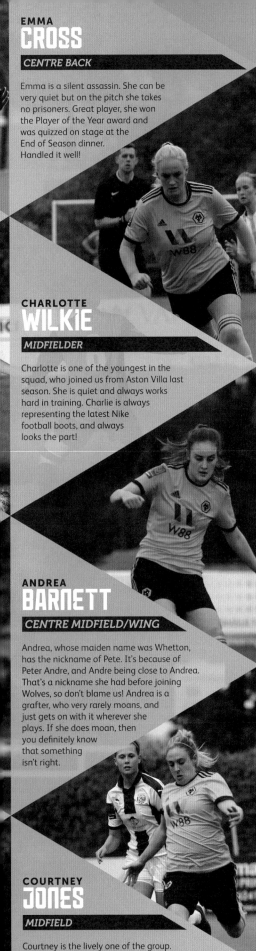
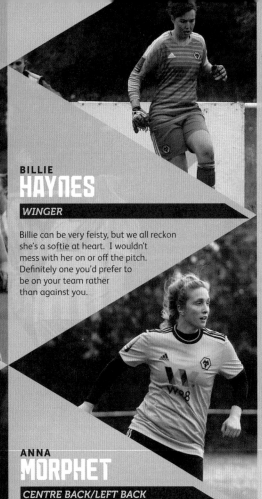

EMMA
CROSS

CENTRE BACK

Emma is a silent assassin. She can be very quiet but on the pitch she takes no prisoners. Great player, she won the Player of the Year award and was quizzed on stage at the End of Season dinner. Handled it well!

CHARLOTTE
WILKIE

MIDFIELDER

Charlotte is one of the youngest in the squad, who joined us from Aston Villa last season. She is quiet and always works hard in training. Charlie is always representing the latest Nike football boots, and always looks the part!

ANDREA
BARNETT

CENTRE MIDFIELD/WING

Andrea, whose maiden name was Whetton, has the nickname of Pete. It's because of Peter Andre, and Andre being close to Andrea. That's a nickname she had before joining Wolves, so don't blame us! Andrea is a grafter, who very rarely moans, and just gets on with it wherever she plays. If she does moan, then you definitely know that something isn't right.

COURTNEY
JONES

MIDFIELD

Courtney is the lively one of the group. Always buzzing around and loves the banter! Great talker on and off the pitch. Last season she got the nickname as the shuffler, because of her little legs shuffling around in midfield.

BILLIE
HAYNES

WINGER

Billie can be very feisty, but we all reckon she's a softie at heart. I wouldn't mess with her on or off the pitch. Definitely one you'd prefer to be on your team rather than against you.

ANNA
MORPHET

CENTRE BACK/LEFT BACK

Possesses a wand of a left foot. A quiet girl, but Anna's delivery from set pieces is as good as it can get. I have a lot to thank her for in terms of setting up my headed goals! A favour for a favour maybe, as I taught Anna A-level PE last year!

JEN
ANSLOW

LEFT BACK/LEFT MIDFIELD

Like me, one of the older, or, shall we say more experienced, members of the squad. Another player with a fantastic left foot, and the sensible one in the squad. Jen loves her coffee too. Whether she is running late or not, when she arrives for training or on a matchday it will usually be with a Costa or a Starbucks.

MADDIE
ELBRO

GOALKEEPER

They say that goalkeepers are crazy don't they? Well Maddie is not at that stage yet! She is only 17 but has a very mature head on her shoulders. She also never stops smiling, and is always positive.

NATALIE
WIDDAL

CENTRE BACK/RIGHT BACK

Another who has won the Player of the Year award not so long ago, Natalie loves the banter and winding people up, including the staff. But it's all in jest. A great team player, she loves the physical side of the game and getting stuck in to a challenge!

We also asked Anna, in the wake of the increased support for Wolves Women from Wolves FC, and England's high-profile World Cup performance, for her thoughts on the rising importance of the ladies' game.

" The big difference for me now is that young girls can aspire to be a professional footballer. When I was younger, there wasn't even a team that I could go to. Now, you hear girls talking about being a professional footballer and it is fantastic. The impact of the media coverage has been huge.

In the past you'd be lucky to hear the women's game even get a short mention but now, thanks to the development of the England team and their performances at major competitions, it is getting far more attention. That helps, and I think with the way the game is progressing, with more girls playing and more qualified coaches involved, the standard is going to get better and better.

Here at Wolves, the standard of the players coming up through the Regional Talent Centres has improved over the last couple of seasons with so much energy, desire and quality. We have also become more integrated into the club, getting involved in kit launches and signing sessions with the men's team, playing a part in the End of Season dinner and now being able to train twice a week at the Sir Jack Hayward Training Ground at Compton. The club could not be in a better place at the moment – and we are both proud and excited to be a part of it. "

WINNERS 2019

ASIA TROPHY

Wolves in China

Pre-season for Wolves in 2019 was that little bit extra special. A first ever trip by the club to China, home of club owners Fosun, who played their part in providing some fantastic hospitality for staff and players during the trip to Nanjing and Shanghai.

On the pitch the trip went perfectly, a 4-0 win in the Asia Cup Trophy Semi Finals against Newcastle followed by victory on penalties against Premier League champions Manchester City in the final after the game finished goalless. A very well-deserved trophy!

Off the pitch there were a huge range of events which the squad took part in, which included getting a valuable insight into the Chinese culture. Events included the launch of the new Wolves Megastore in Shanghai, a fashion show, sharing a beer with Wolves legend Steve Bull, a 'They Wore The Shirt' exhibition, Wolves Foundation coaching, a session of Taiji, and much more.

A great visit to cement relations between Wolves and Fosun and set things up for the new campaign.

Young Wolves

Official Wolves Junior
MEMBERSHIPS
SEASON 2019/20

Wolves Dribblers AGES 0 TO 3
£12.00

EXCLUSIVE GIFTS

Includes:
- Exclusive plate, fork, spoon & 2 bandana bibs
- Signed certificate from head coach
- Exclusive events
- **Plus lots more!**

tickets.wolves.co.uk/memberships | 0371 222 1877

IT WAS A GREAT PREMIER LEAGUE SEASON FOR WOLVES IN 2018/19, & ANOTHER PREMIER SEASON FOR THE YOUNG WOLVES, WITH THE CLUB'S FANS OF THE FUTURE ENJOYING ALL THE BENEFITS OF THEIR ANNUAL MEMBERSHIP.

So many events and fun competitions, giveaways, and above all, so many chances to meet and mingle with their heroes. Here are a few reminders of another fantastic year for Young Wolves...

Young Wolves — AGES 4 TO 11
£15.00

EXCLUSIVE GIFTS

Includes:
- 100 loyalty points
- Exclusive member events
- Discounts from selected partners
- Opportunity to claim one of 5,000 FREE tickets to be available to junior members across this season
- **Plus lots more!**

#Wolf Pack — AGES 12 TO 16
£17.50

EXCLUSIVE GIFTS

Includes:
- 100 loyalty points
- Exclusive member events
- Discounts from selected partners
- Opportunity to claim one of 5,000 FREE tickets to be available to junior members across this season
- **Plus lots more!**

39

WOLFIE'S FUN PAGE

40

Spot the Difference

Can you find the 6 differences between these two pictures?

Howlers...

Why was the footballer upset on their birthday?

Because they received a red card!

Did you know?

In 1979, a Scottish Cup tie between Falkirk and Inverness Caley Thistle had to be postponed a whopping twenty-nine times due to bad weather.

The face-off!

Photos of three Wolves players have been mixed up! Can you tell who they are from their national flags?

1
2
3

Con-crest!

We've merged the Wolves crest with those of two other Season 19/20 Premier League clubs – do you know which?

Can you finish this picture of the tunnel?

Use the grid to help you mirror the image!

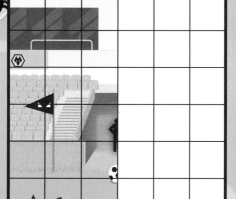

Did you know?

The first ever live coverage of a match on TV was Arsenal versus Arsenal reserves in 1937.

COLOUR ME IN!

Howlers...

Which football team loves ice cream?

Aston Vanilla!

Scrambled Shirts!

The letters have been mixed up on these shirts. Can you figure out which players they belong to?

JEEZNIM

TROPIICA

JONNY CASTRO OTTO

Did you know?

Neil Armstrong wanted to take a football to the moon, but NASA refused on the grounds that football (or 'soccer') was un-American.

Answers on page 61

WHO ARE YA?

For the final quiz in this year's Annual, we are concentrating on the Wolves squad of players from the 2018/19 season.

How much do you know about their backgrounds? And their performances over the campaign? We've helped out with options for each question – and all the answers are on page 61.

1 Which summer signing wore squad number 11 for the 2018/19 season?

A Joao Moutinho B Rui Patricio C Raul Jimenez

2 Which Wolves player was part of the 2012 Olympic winning team when Britain hosted the games?

A Raul Jimenez B Willy Boly C Jonny Otto

3 Which player made his full international debut during the season – against England?

A Ruben Neves B Diogo Jota C Jonny Otto

4 Which player scored his only Premier League goal of the season at Wembley?

A Jonny Otto B Romain Saiss C Helder Costa

5 Against whom did Ivan Cavaleiro score with his first touch in the Premier League?

A Burnley B Southampton C Bournemouth

6 Against which team did Wolves post their highest league attendance of the season?

A Arsenal B Manchester United C Everton

7 In what minute did Ruben Neves score Wolves' first goal of the campaign?

A 44 B 39 C 34

8 Which Spanish team did Wolves beat in their only home pre-season friendly?

A Real Betis B Real Sociedad C Villarreal

9 Which Wolves player has previously scored in a Europa League quarter final v Manchester United?

A Leander Dendoncker B Diogo Jota C Joao Moutinho

10 Who equalised for Wolves against Tottenham at Wembley?

A Raul Jimenez B Willy Boly C Diogo Jota

41

 Wolves Academy

HOMEGROWN HERO

MORGAN
Gibbs-White

DION
Sanderson

MAXIMILIAN
Kilman

TAYLOR
Perry

 Wolves Academy

THREE TO WATCH

A WHOLE
JOTA
LOVE

BOLY
GOOD!

KING HENRY!

We always try and catch up with a former player in the Wolves Annual, and we didn't have to travel too far to track this fella down.

Karl Henry was born and brought up in Wolverhampton – Ashmore Park to be precise – and has stayed in the Midlands with his family since his playing career came to an end.

It's just over ten years since Henry lifted the Championship trophy with Wolves, going on to represent his home town club in the Premier League, part of a career which saw 574 senior appearances. As he reveals in our Q&A below, he is also still very much in touch with all things Wolves and Wolverhampton, and is all set to play a key role in the club's activities in the community.

Starting from the beginning Karl, how did you first come to be signed by Wolves?
I was at Stoke where I had been since I was young and in their Academy. I wasn't playing regularly, and was ready for a new challenge and ready to leave, but because I was still under 24, I couldn't just go on a free transfer even though I was at the end of my contract. At the time I had agreed to go and join QPR , and they were just trying to agree a deal without having to go to a tribunal. My agent had brought Jay Bothroyd to Wolves at that time, and spoke to Mick McCarthy about me as well. All of a sudden, I get called up to Stoke manager Tony Pulis's office on a Friday afternoon, to say that Mick had phoned him.

So Wolves were interested in signing you?
It seemed that way, although it was still early stages. Mick had asked if I could go and play in a training game on the pitch. Well yes, definitely! I got off the phone and rang my old man to tell him. It was only when he told me that I discovered it wasn't just any training game. It was a friendly against Aston Villa, as part of Steve Bull's testimonial, 20 years after he had signed for the club. A big crowd was expected, and it all felt a bit surreal. I started calling up a few friends. 'Guess where I am playing tomorrow?'

And how did it go?
Well Mick spoke to me before the game and said he was going to put me on for the second half. I presumed I would then train with the team the week after and see what happened. As it was, very early into the game, unfortunately Mark Davies got injured. Mick just told me I was going on, and it was probably good that I didn't have much time to think about it – no time to get stressed! I went on, and had the game of my life. I remember I was running around the pitch, smashing everyone! There was no such thing as a friendly when you were trying to win a contract with your home town club. I couldn't let that opportunity pass.

And it worked?
Yes it did! Mick said after the game that he wanted to offer me a contract, and that was music to my ears. I have no idea how it ended with QPR – and the Wolves deal wasn't as good as that one – but 100 per cent, I wanted to move to Molineux. I signed as soon as I could, and was delighted!

And the rest is history?

Yes. I went on to spend seven years with Wolves. Some ups and downs but I really enjoyed it. I think we really over-achieved to reach the play-offs in that first season when Mick, Taff (Ian Evans) and TC (Terry Connor) pretty much had to rebuild the whole squad with very little money and then we only just missed out on the top six the following year. Then of course came the 2008/09 season...

Ah yes. The Championship-winning season. How do you remember that one and what was it like to lift that trophy with Jody Craddock?

I think we had the foundations from the previous two years and then the signings that summer – David Jones, Richard Stearman, Chris Iwelumo and Sam Vokes – helped move us on. We had such a good group at the time and when I look back now that is what stands out. With some of the dressing rooms I have been in since, I think we all took for granted what a great group of people we had at that time. It is no surprise that so many of us have stayed in touch. That doesn't happen by accident either. It is how Mick put it all together with good players and good people who were hungry for success, including a mixture of youth and experience.

Any particular highlights from the season?

I remember that Nottingham Forest game early on when we won 5-1. I think we were unplayable that day and it was a standout performance so early in the season. Ipswich away early on as well, Charlton, Preston with Chris Iwelumo's hat trick. There were so many really professional performances and then of course the finish we had with the wins against Derby and QPR were brilliant memories. As captain of my hometown club, to lift that trophy in what was my first major career achievement was incredible.

You then got to play for Wolves in the Premier League and there were plenty more ups and downs over the following years before you left?

The Premier League was a fantastic challenge. It is the pinnacle for any footballer, the best league in the world where everyone wants to play. Maybe we were all in awe of it a little bit at first, but then it became so enjoyable. We were taking on some of the best teams in the world, and sometimes beating them, results and performances I will never forget. The relegation was tough to take, and then the second one as well. It is never any disgrace to be relegated from the Premier League, but we should never have gone down again, and we all have to take responsibility for that, myself included. It made for a sour end to my career, which was disappointing, because I always gave everything for the club. I think over the passing of time hopefully that group of players can be remembered for what we achieved in getting the club into the Premier League, and staying there, before everything started to go so wrong.

Finally, you have been back in touch with Wolves and the area again recently, with a rather special role you are now taking on...

Yes. With my playing days over I am now concentrating on business interests that I set up towards the end of my career. But I have been delighted to become Wolves Foundation's first ever Ambassador and am looking forward to helping out with some of the community projects, so important for a football club. I have also got more involved with the Former Players' Association and was delighted to attend their annual dinner and take part in a visit to the Good Shepherd Soup Kitchen. It is nice to be back involved a little bit because Wolves was – and still is – such a big part of my life. I still have a lot of personal pride and honour in what I achieved at Wolves and what we achieved as a team, and have a sense of nostalgia when I come back to Molineux. Wolves gave me and my family such great times and experiences which I will never, ever forget.

Foundation

The official charity of Wolverhampton Wanderers FC

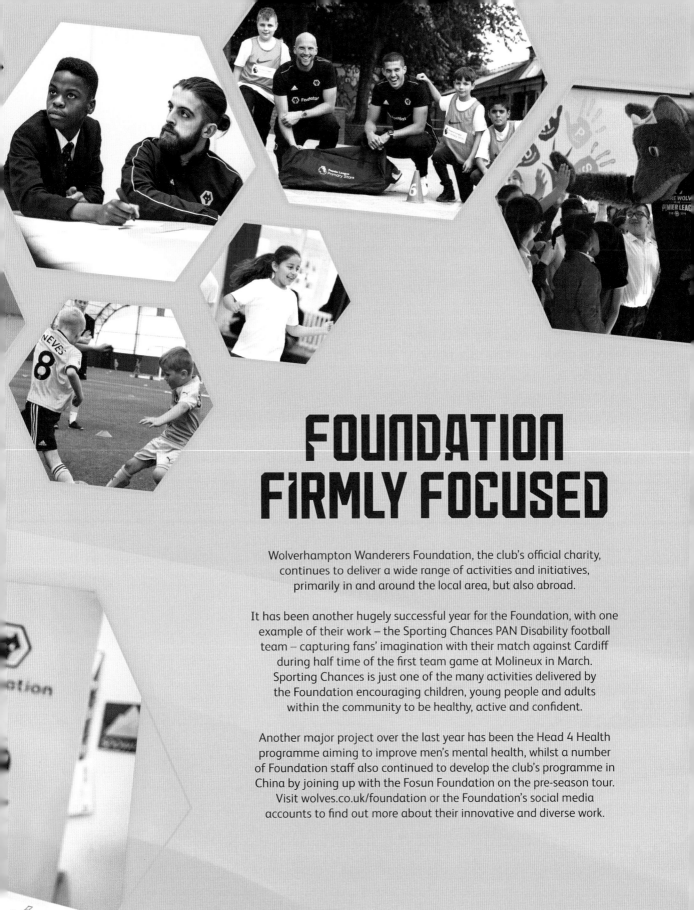

FOUNDATION FIRMLY FOCUSED

Wolverhampton Wanderers Foundation, the club's official charity, continues to deliver a wide range of activities and initiatives, primarily in and around the local area, but also abroad.

It has been another hugely successful year for the Foundation, with one example of their work – the Sporting Chances PAN Disability football team – capturing fans' imagination with their match against Cardiff during half time of the first team game at Molineux in March. Sporting Chances is just one of the many activities delivered by the Foundation encouraging children, young people and adults within the community to be healthy, active and confident.

Another major project over the last year has been the Head 4 Health programme aiming to improve men's mental health, whilst a number of Foundation staff also continued to develop the club's programme in China by joining up with the Fosun Foundation on the pre-season tour. Visit wolves.co.uk/foundation or the Foundation's social media accounts to find out more about their innovative and diverse work.

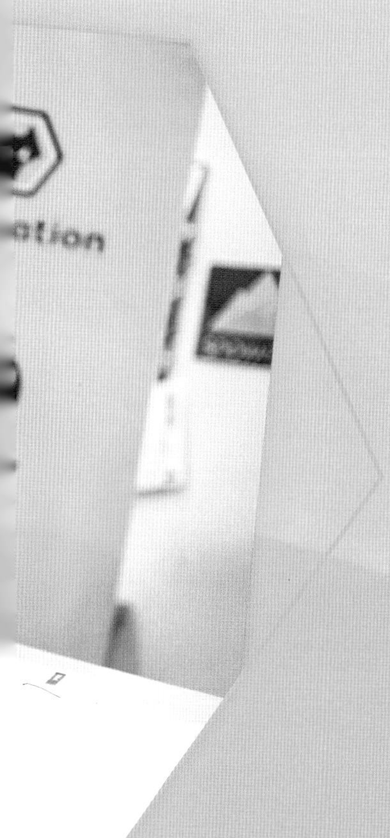

Foundation

wolves.co.uk/foundation

@wwfcfoundation

JESUS VALLEJO

Jesus Vallejo was the first new face to arrive in the summer transfer window, joining on a season-long loan from the mighty Real Madrid.

Vallejo, who started his career with Real Zaragoza, has been part of the Madrid squad which has won a series of honours, as well as captaining Spain Under-21s to the 2019 European Championships.

Real Madrid recommended me a lot to come here, because **WOLVES DID AN INCREDIBLE JOB** last season, and I hope to do the same – **I am very happy to be here.**

Jesus Vallejo

PATRICK CUTRONE

Exciting young striker Patrick Cutrone checked in from AC Milan having come through the ranks at the Italian giants, a club he joined at the age of just nine.

Cutrone is also a full Italy international, making his debut for the senior team in 2018 after appearing at every level of youth football for his country.

I'M VERY PLEASED TO BE HERE because the club really wanted me. I'm very happy and I want to **give my all for the team** AND CAN'T WAIT TO GET STARTED.

Patrick Cutrone

Wolves eSports

WOLVES GOING FOR
eSports gold

Wolves have enjoyed an exciting year in the world of eSports, which continues to prove an ever-growing industry with millions taking to their consoles all over the world.

Since partnering with Bundled, one of Europe's leading console gaming eSports agencies, the club has been able to really step up its efforts to engage with fans in new and exciting ways. Over the year this has included getting involved in many different eSports events at home and abroad, including forming a new eSports team in China. Plus, in the summer of 2019, Wolves were the only Premier League team to qualify with representation at the FIFA eWorld Cup Grand Final, at the O2 in London.

Wolves' two Brazilian players – Fifilza (Flavio Brito) and Ebinho (Ebinho Bernardes da Costa Filho) – came through from a competition featuring over 40 million gamers worldwide to make the final 32 which qualified for the event. The Wolves Annual caught up with Ebinho (Xbox) and Flavio (PlayStation) to find out a bit more about them.

Ebinho:

When did you start playing eSports?
I started playing eSports in 2016, when there was a tournament here in my city. I went to play and ended up being champion. From then on I started to play some championships but I only dedicated myself 100% to it in 2018.

How do you feel representing Wolves at eSports?
It is a great pleasure to be able to represent Wolves, a club that has been growing incredibly on the world football scene and I trust my work. I just have to thank everyone who made it possible, as I am very privileged and I know that many people would like to be in my place. So I will do my best, always.

What is your best achievement in eSports so far?
I think I have some important accomplishments for me. To represent a major world football club like Wolves, to be the first representative of the Brazilian national team in a world cup and to play the FIFA eWorld Cup in my first year of international tournaments, it is very difficult to choose one.

Who is your favourite Wolves player?
Ruben Neves is a player that I have been watching for some time and when I went to Molineux to watch a match, he had a great performance.

What's your tip for young eSports players?
Never give up, I think this is the main tip. I always had the dream of playing international tournaments and for two years I couldn't, but I never gave up and when the opportunity came I gave my best. So the biggest tip is: Never give up, you are capable of everything.

What are your aims for the future?
My big dream is to be world champion, I will continue dedicating myself to one day reach this goal. Today, my biggest goal is to be my best version and represent my country and my team in the best possible way.

Photos courtesy of EA Sports.

Flavio:

When did you first start playing eSports?
I started to play eSports when it was Fifa 17, in the beginning of the FUT Champions cup.

What is your best achievement so far?
My best achievement so far is to have reached the top four of the play-offs and the top ten in the world.

How do you feel about representing Wolves?
I feel really good about it, and also comfortable. Wolves give me all the support that I need.

Who is your favourite Wolves player?
Diogo Jota.

What's your tip for young eSports players?
Never give up, and train hard. I think dedication is the most important thing.

What are your aims for the future?
I want to be a champion and the best PS4 player that there is.

Pat & Dave's WOLVES MUSEUM mini-tour

The Wolves Museum continues to prove a popular attraction for fans of all ages with a variety of attractions from fun games right through to unique memorabilia.

Let's take a mini-tour with archivist Pat Quirke and Museum Assistant Dave Jones.

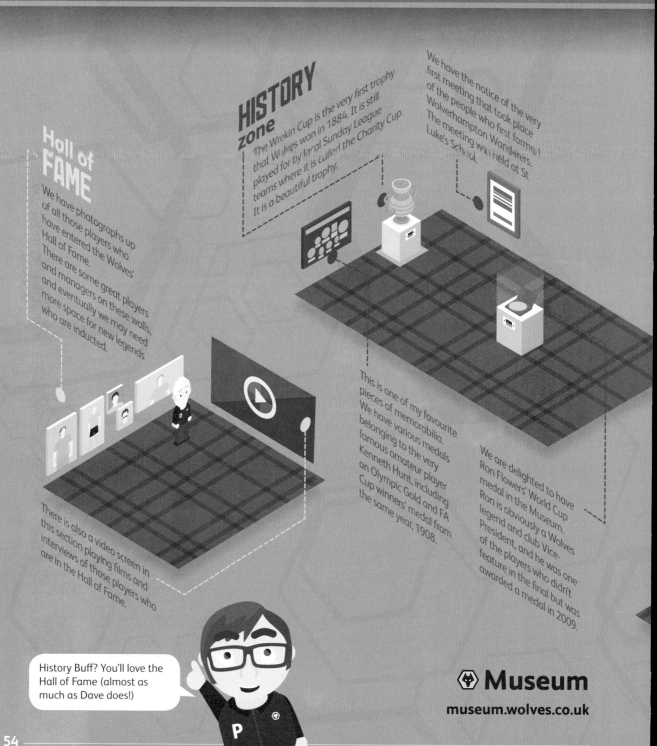

HISTORY zone

The Wrekin Cup is the very first trophy that Wolves won in 1884. It is still played for by local Sunday League teams where it is called the Charity Cup. It is a beautiful trophy.

We have the notice of the very first meeting that took place of the people who first formed Wolverhampton Wanderers. The meeting was held at St Luke's School.

Hall of FAME

We have photographs up of all those players who have entered the Wolves' Hall of Fame. There are some great players and managers on these walls, and eventually we may need more space for new legends who are inducted.

There is also a video screen in this section playing films and interviews of those players who are in the Hall of Fame.

This is one of my favourite pieces of memorabilia. We have various medals belonging to the very famous amateur player Kenneth Hunt, including an Olympic Gold and FA Cup winners' medal from the same year, 1908.

We are delighted to have Ron Flowers' World Cup medal in the Museum. Ron is obviously a Wolves legend and club Vice-President, and he was one of the players who didn't feature in the final but was awarded a medal in 2009.

History Buff? You'll love the Hall of Fame (almost as much as Dave does!)

⬡ Museum
museum.wolves.co.uk

P Welcome to our miniature Wolves Museum!

D Here, Pat and I will be showing you some of our favourite parts of the Wolves Museum. Come and visit us at the real Museum, or join us for a Sunday tour!

GAME zone

'Beat the Keeper' is a chance to test your reactions on another state-of-the-art interactive game. Are your instincts and movements fast enough to be a goalkeeper yourself?

CLUB zone

We have a small cinema-style room in the Club Zone with a big screen which tells the story of Wolves through the good days and the bad days, right through until more recent times.

If you can kick it anywhere near the net, you've beaten Pat's attempt!

Dave, I told you that was a practise shot!

We have photographs and information relating to the many players who have come through the Wolves Academy and gone on to play for the club, and also elsewhere. This includes players like Robbie Keane and Joleon Lescott who went on to achieve great things.

We also have a section on Sports Science, in which we look at how progress in this area has had an impact on football.

The Game Zone offers visitors the chance to take on challenges which are part of football. This includes taking penalties against some of the club's more iconic goalkeepers, from Bert Williams through to Matt Murray.

Wolverhampton Wanderers plays such a vital role in the local community, and the club's history is linked to the heritage of the city. It is a great story, which needs to be told, and the Museum is a fantastic way of doing just that. We are very proud of what we have on offer here for supporters.

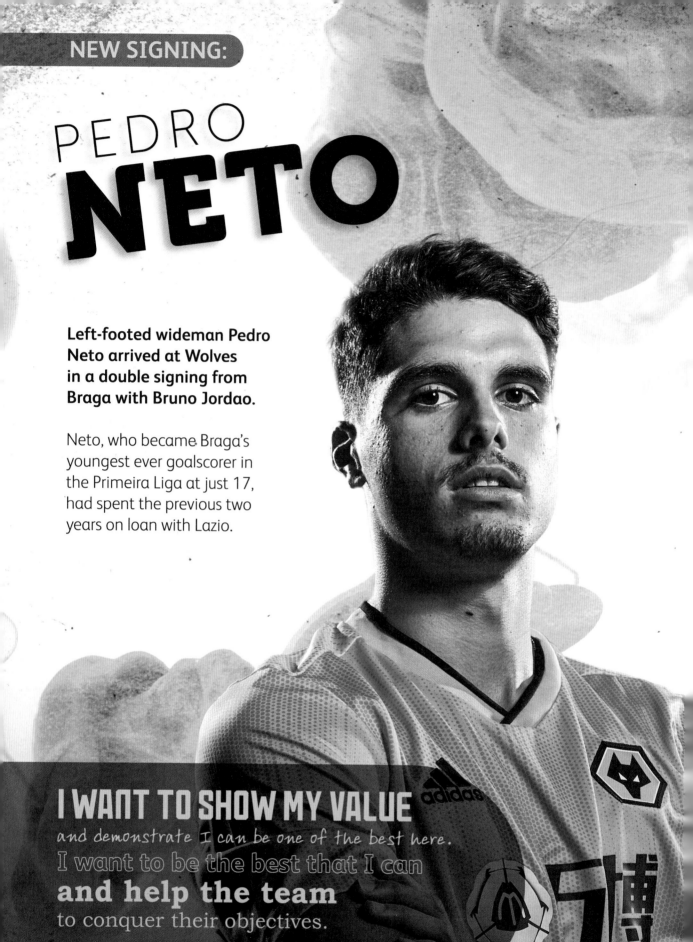

PEDRO NETO

Left-footed wideman Pedro Neto arrived at Wolves in a double signing from Braga with Bruno Jordao.

Neto, who became Braga's youngest ever goalscorer in the Primeira Liga at just 17, had spent the previous two years on loan with Lazio.

I WANT TO SHOW MY VALUE

and demonstrate I can be one of the best here. I want to be the best that I can **and help the team** to conquer their objectives.

Pedro Neto

BRUNO JORDAO

Midfielder Bruno Jordao first came to prominence in Portugal with Uniao De Leiria, coming through their youth ranks and then scoring four goals in 23 appearances in their first team at the age of just 16.

Jordao then moved to Braga, and on to a two-year loan at Lazio, before making the switch to Molineux along with Pedro Neto.

I know Wolves is a big team, with **big dreams.** **I'M VERY PLEASED TO BE HERE –** When I knew it was an opportunity to come here, **I said yes with no doubts, so I'm very happy AND PROUD TO BE HERE.**

Bruno Jordao

PLAYER

Matt
DOHERTY
#2

Position: **Defender**
Apps: **252** Goals: **21**

Jesus
VALLEJO
#4

Position: **Defender**
Apps: **0** Goals: **0**

Pedro
NETO
#7

Position: **Midfielder**
Apps: **0** Goals: **0**

Ruben
NEVES
#8

Position: **Midfielder**
Apps: **82** Goals: **11**

Rui
PATRICIO
#11

Position: **Goalkeeper**
Apps: **37** Goals: **0**

Willy
BOLY
#15

Position: **Defender**
Apps: **78** Goals: **7**

Diogo
JOTA
#18

Position: **Forward**
Apps: **83** Goals: **28**

Jonny
OTTO
#19

Position: **Defender**
Apps: **39** Goals: **1**

Joao
MOUTINHO
#28

Position: **Midfielder**
Apps: **44** Goals: **1**

Ruben
VINAGRE
#29

Position: **Defender**
Apps: **34** Goals: **1**

Maximilian
KILMAN
#49

Position: **Defender**
Apps: **1** Goals: **0**

PROFILES

#5

Ryan
BENNETT
Position: **Defender**
Apps: **74** Goals: **2**

#6

Bruno
JORDAO
Position: **Midfielder**
Apps: **0** Goals: **0**

#9

Raul
JIMENEZ
Position: **Forward**
Apps: **44** Goals: **17**

#10

Patrick
CUTRONE
Position: **Forward**
Apps: **0** Goals: **0**

#16

Conor
COADY
Position: **Defender**
Apps: **178** Goals: **2**

#17

Morgan
GIBBS-WHITE
Position: **Midfielder**
Apps: **54** Goals: **0**

#21

John
RUDDY
Position: **Goalkeeper**
Apps: **54** Goals: **0**

#27

Romain
SAISS
Position: **Defender/Midfielder**
Apps: **95** Goals: **6**

#32

Leander
DENDONCKER
Position: **Defender/Midfielder**
Apps: **26** Goals: **2**

#37

Adama
TRAORE
Position: **Midfielder**
Apps: **36** Goals: **1**

Please note all appearances/goals figures are for all competitions for Wolves,
and correct as at the end of the 2018/19 season.
Squad list compiled of senior players at the club (and not loaned out) at start of 2019/20 campaign.

A **KIT** FIT FOR THE PREM!

Here are the new home, away and goalkeeping kits Wolves are wearing in the 2019/20 season.

The home kit was launched at a special event at Wolves' Megastore, with the away kit, a return to black shirts and shorts, officially revealed at the club's new Shanghai Megastore during the pre-season trip to China.

NOW AVAILABLE
WOLVES X ADIDAS
IN STORE & ONLINE

shop.wolves.co.uk

THE ANSWERS...

PAGE 40

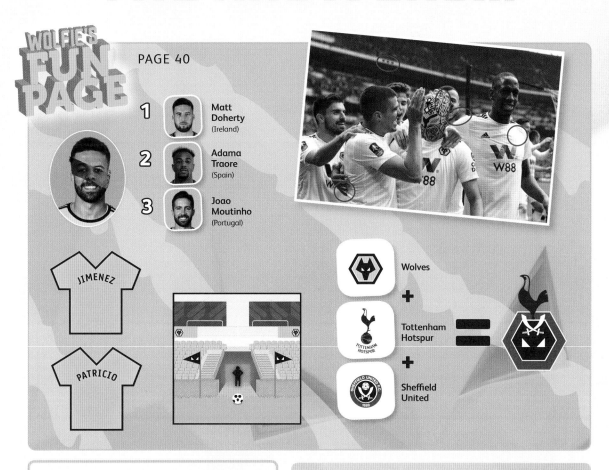

1 Matt Doherty (Ireland)

2 Adama Traore (Spain)

3 Joao Moutinho (Portugal)

JIMENEZ

PATRICIO

Wolves
+
Tottenham Hotspur
+
Sheffield United
=

Enjoyed this year's puzzles?
Follow us on social media **@YoungWolves** to take part in more fun and exclusive competitions!

A PREMIER WORDSEARCH!

PAGE 29

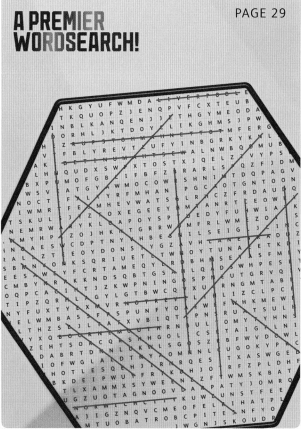

WHO ARE YA?

PAGE 41

1 B Rui Patricio

2 A Raul Jimenez

3 C Jonny Otto

4 C Helder Costa

5 B Southampton

6 A Arsenal

7 A 44

8 C Villarreal

9 A Leander Dendoncker

10 B Willy Boly

THE NUMBERS GAME

PAGE 28

1 Steve Sedgley

2 Colin Cameron

3 Henri Camara

4 Kenny Miller

5 Wayne Hennessey

6 Nenad Milijas

7 Emmanuel Frimpong

8 Sam Ricketts

9 Conor Coady

10 Leo Bonatini

Where's Wolfie?

Wolfie has hidden somewhere amongst the Wolves supporters! Can you find him?